THE HUNGARIANS IN AMERICA

THE **HUNGARIANS** IN AMERICA

REZSOE and MARGARET GRACZA

*Photo Selection
and Captions by*
MIRIAM BUTWIN

Published by
Lerner Publications Company
Minneapolis, Minnesota

. . . CONTENTS . . .

Statue of St. Stephen, on the Fishers Bastion, Budapest. The first king of Hungary, Stephen ruled from 1001 until 1038. Following his father's lead, Stephen unified and Christianized the Magyar tribes. His crown became a symbol of the Hungarian nation, and Stephen, its patron saint.

Introduction

American Hungarians have a rich and heroic heritage. Their origins and their language are unique, and their history of more than 1,000 years is unusually complex and dramatic.

In Europe, Hungarians are ethnically separate; they are neither Slavic nor Germanic nor Latin. They are related only to the Finns and Estonians and that by an ancient connection. Hungarians are descendants of the Magyars, a nomadic tribe that developed in the Eurasian wilderness and steppe during the first 1,000 years A.D.

The Hungarian language, also called Magyar, stands alone. It is considered a difficult language to learn. It is phonetic, precise, and musical. Being phonetic, it is spelled as it sounds, so spelling lessons are unknown. Magyar is particularly adapted to poetry and the expression of fine shades of meaning.

The land that the Magyar tribes staked out 1,000 years ago was fertile and strategic. Most of their miseries came about when alien forces also wanted the use of this land. Repeatedly the Magyars opposed an outside force which was either invading, occupying, plundering, or oppressing them. They were often engaged in a struggle for survival.

Historical experience has made the Hungarian character resilient, resourceful, and always original. Ultimate values mean a great deal to the Hungarian, and he puts a high price on individual excellence.

Their heritage and history remain important to Hungarians who have become Americans. The story of who emigrated from Hungary, when, and why is linked directly to historical events in Hungary and America, but mainly in Hungary.

PART I

The First Hungarians
in America

1. *A Hungarian Crewman and Leif Ericson*

A Hungarian, it is told, took part in the discovery of America. In the year 1000 A.D., the Hungarian was one of 35 crew members who landed with the Norwegian, Leif Ericson, on the eastern coast of North America. This Hungarian is supposed to have provided Leif Ericson with a name for the new land. How did a Hungarian happen to be linked with a Norwegian expedition?

In the Scandinavian saga called Chronicle of the Kings of Norway, or *Heimskringla,* there is an incident about a Hungarian called Tyrker. The day after Leif Ericson's boat arrived on the new shore, Leif noticed that Tyrker was missing. Leif went ashore with a party to search for the "stubby, ugly but dexterous man." Leif found him merry and excited.

Tyrker "babbled in Turkish" and could not be understood by Leif and his search party. Tyrker realized that they didn't understand him so he spoke to them in their own language: "I have found wine and grapes. I came from a land in which wine and grapes are abundant." From this incident Leif Ericson received his inspiration. He named the shore "Vinland," or in English, "Wineland." The name persists today as Leif Ericson's name for America.

What proof have we that Tyrker was Hungarian? The saga records that he was little in size and a South Countryman. These are two possible clues. A third is the fact that he was called Tyrker. And this is the biggest clue to his identity. In Icelandic, Tyrker means Turk. If Tyrker was called this because he was a Turk, how could he be a Hungarian? It is assumed that he had another name of his own.

Oddly enough, it is proof to many scholars that Tyrker was Hungarian. Scholars know from records of the tenth century that Hungarians were referred to as Turks.[*]

Another proof that Tyrker was Hungarian and not Turkish is the fact that Hungarians of the tenth century were in friendly communication with the Northmen. They shared a love for bravery and a hunger for adventure. The Hungarians served as soldiers with the Northmen. It is known that they fought in 971 as mercenaries in the army of a Scandinavian prince. In that year the prince waged war against Constantinople and lost. It is easy to conjecture, then, that many of his mercenaries fled with the other Northmen. One of them could have been Tyrker, who went far enough north to join the crew of Leif Ericson.

[*] Some legends suggest that Tyrker was a German. It is not known if the Turks have considered claiming him.

St. Stephen (right) and his son **Prince Emericus.** The young prince died in a hunting accident and was canonized with his father late in the eleventh century.

Amerigo Vespucci (1451-1512), Italian navigator, explored the coast of South America in 1499 and in 1501. His name, of Hungarian origin, was given to the new continent in 1507.

2. *The Name America and a Hungarian Saint*

Leif Ericson had a name for the continent of America but Christopher Columbus did not. Actually the name America was suggested by a German geographer after Columbus's time. It is believed that indirectly and by way of Italy a Hungarian saint contributed to this name.

The Hungarian St. Emeric was popular with the Italians. In 1451 Nastagio Vespucci, a notary of Florence, named his new son Amerigo Vespucci after the Hungarian saint. In Italian the word Emeric becomes Amerigo.

Amerigo Vespucci grew up to be a famous navigator and explorer of America. The German geographer, Martin Waldseemuller, suggested his name for the new country in a pamphlet published in 1507. From Imre to Emeric to Amerigo to America, a Hungarian name was linked to the naming of America.

3. An English Expedition and a Hungarian Scholar

During the sixteenth century, a Hungarian took part in a colonizing voyage to America. About this particular voyage and about this Hungarian there is no dispute. The story is well documented by the British historian, Richard Hakluyt. The voyage in 1583 was an attempt to colonize the new land "not possessed by any Christian prince or people." It was directed by Queen Elizabeth of England. The Englishman in charge was Sir Humphrey Gilbert.

When Sir Humphrey was planning his voyage and organizing his crew, a man of letters was introduced to him. He was a Hungarian, and true to Renaissance fashion, he had a Latin name, Parmenius. He was a poet, a scholar, and a humanist. Sir Humphrey liked him, and hired him for his crew.

Sir Humphrey Gilbert, scroll in hand, claims Newfoundland for Queen Elizabeth of England, August 1583. Among Sir Humphrey's men was Parmenius, a Hungarian scholar.

His duty was to be the chronicler, the official historian of the voyage. Versed in classical poetry, he was to give the chronicles style and elegance which could be understood and appreciated by all educated Europeans of that era. Therefore, he wrote in Latin and not in Hungarian or English.

The fact that he wrote in Latin explains, in part, how he happened to be in England. As a scholar and humanist, he was not welcome in his own country at that time. The Ottoman Turks occupied Hungary, and they had little tolerance for a learned Christian. It was natural for a man like Parmenius to seek the greater freedom of England for the development of his studies.

The part Parmenius played in history was certain but brief. On the return trip two months later the ship was caught in a violent storm and he was killed. Fortunately his chronicle survived the voyage.

4. *A Colonel in George Washington's Army*

Two centuries later, a Hungarian military man distinguished himself in the American Revolution, which found great sympathy in Europe. Large numbers applied to come over and help the colonies fight for their freedom from English rule. When Benjamin Franklin was in France on official business in 1776, he received a stream of applications for the American army. One of the applications was from a Hungarian hussar officer, Michael Kovats.

Kovats's application was rejected in Paris, but this did not deter him. He came to America on his own, and immediately contacted a general who applied for him directly to George Washington. His application was eventually reviewed and accepted.

The general Kovats had contacted was the Pole, Casimir Pulaski, who had been assigned to organize the cavalry. Pulaski needed help badly, and a Hungarian hussar could be very useful. Hussars were crack military men, specialists in cavalry skills.

Although there was public pressure against making foreigners high-ranking officers, Washington appointed Kovats a colonel.

Michael Kovats helped to organize and train the cavalry to such a level of efficiency that even the enemy praised it as "the best Cavalry the rebels ever had." And it was the enemy that took his life. He died in battle May 11, 1779, when his outfit, the Pulaski Legion, was heavily outnumbered. At that stage of the war, the British were menacing Charleston, South Carolina, and the Legion had been sent to give some hope to the city.

Colonel Kovats was one of the 141 Hungarians who fought in the Revolution under the American flag. Many Hungarians fought under the French flag, since they were enlisted in the contingent sent by the French king to help the revolutionaries.

5. A Hungarian Writer Discovers America for His Countrymen

In the early nineteenth century, Europeans asked endless questions about democracy and the new nation. How did a melting pot work? Could men really govern themselves? What effect did democracy have on family life and religion? What effect did it have on business and labor, law and art, manners and morals?

One Hungarian who helped answer some of these questions for his countrymen was a nobleman named Alexander Farkas de Boloni. He traveled around America in 1831, the same year as the famous French writer, Alexis de Tocqueville. Both men watched democracy at work and each published a book about it in his homeland.

Both men were highly observant. They had keen eyes and sharp, analytical minds, and tried to penetrate beneath the surface of American life. De Tocqueville's book, *American Democracy*, written in French and translated into many languages, became a worldwide classic. De Boloni's book, *Journey in North America*, was written in Hungarian and became important only in Hungary. It was not translated into English or any other language. Both books are written in an enjoyable style and many of their impressions and conclusions hold true today.

For many Hungarians, de Boloni's book held up the New World as a guiding light. In fact, the book had considerable influence in the Hungarian reform era. That era culminated in the Revolution of 1848-49, a war against the ruling Austrian House of Hapsburg.

Augustus Haraszthy
(1821-1869)

6. A Versatile Pioneer

Another Hungarian traveler who wrote about America was Augustus Haraszthy. He was so impressed by the dynamic life in America that he went back to Hungary in 1842 to fetch his family before returning to stay. In his book he wrote to his countrymen: "Nothing daunts the American . . . the boundless energy and self-assurance are truly breathtaking. He seems to live twice the span of others and to accomplish a hundred times more."

These words may also describe Haraszthy. His career in America was energetic, varied, and colorful. A handsome man, he was skilled in social ways and managed to meet many prominent Americans, including Daniel Webster and President Tyler. Haraszthy was also a very practical, enterprising man.

In Wisconsin Haraszthy put his practical skills to work. He was a builder, a storekeeper, and a steamboat and ferry owner. He made his own firebricks with his own kiln and planted the first hops in Wisconsin. He also became a civic leader. He directed an association which sponsored new citizens, and was a leader in the Wisconsin Historical Society.

Then in true pioneer spirit he crossed the country in a prairie wagon and settled in California. There he had careers as a sheriff, a legislator, a coin melter and refiner, a banker, and most important of all, a viticulturist—an expert in cultivating vineyards. As a viticulturist he made his largest and most important contribution to America. He was the father of the California wine industry and introduced several varieties of grapes native to Hungary. To enrich his contribution he left a large and valuable book on the subject, published in English in 1862.

His other book, published in Hungarian, was a contribution to his native country. Like de Boloni's book, it influenced the democratic movement in Hungary. Although the two books had the same title, they were not repetitive. De Boloni's book (1834) dealth more with ideas, and the subjects of politics and education. Haraszthy's book, published in 1844, was about practical daily life in nineteenth century America.

PART II

Soldiers and Heroes

1. *Lajos Kossuth — Champion of Liberty*

While Hungarians read Boloni's and Haraszthy's books, another writer on democracy was gaining importance — a Hungarian who told his people about freedom and justice. Lajos Kossuth (1802-1894) was a great freedom fighter whose destiny involved America in a profound way.

Kossuth believed deeply in the spirit of democracy. He could express his ideas in powerful, eloquent words. And he had a magnetic personality. These gifts and his skill as a lawyer and statesman were directed toward one end — self-rule for his people. He was the leader of the Hungarian Revolution of 1848, the year of revolutions.

Europeans were not as fortunate in their attempts at revolution as the Americans, who had many conditions in their favor. Americans had the advantages of geography, a refugee past, the pioneer tradition. They had assistance from a large power. The king of France had given support to America with arms, money, and men.

Like other Europeans in revolt, the Hungarians had enormous obstacles to overcome. Their geography was a disadvantage. They had to contend with a feudal system of landownership, and religious jealousies. And perhaps most of all they had to resist the power of an absolute monarchy. By the mid-nineteenth century, some European kings still believed they were responsible to God alone for their acts. To them monarchy was the only form of government. Anything else was anarchy, which to a ruler implied total disorder and lawlessness.

16

Prince Klemens von Metternich (1773-1859) dominated European politics from the downfall of Napoleon in 1815 until the revolutions of 1848. As foreign minister of Austria, he maintained the power of the Hapsburg monarchy by suppressing liberal and nationalist groups within the empire. In 1848, after an uprising in Vienna, he resigned and fled to England.

The monarchy that Hungary had to deal with was centered in Vienna. It was the Austrian House of Hapsburg, which had ruled Hungary since the 1430's when a Hungarian king's daughter married a Hapsburg. For several centuries Hungary had been under Hapsburg rule, usually to the latter's advantage. Hungarians nevertheless maintained their own traditions and language.

By the mid-nineteenth century, a generation after the French Revolution, the urge to get rid of despotic governments had spread from a few revolutionary leaders to large segments of the population. Weary of inequalities, this reform generation found a leader in Lajos Kossuth. He had been sentenced to a prison term because of his sharp criticism of the actions of the Hungarian Diet, which he had attended as a secretary to a delegate. His critical handwritten notes were circulated from door to door by his friends. Even this simple act was considered treasonous and he was tried and convicted.

After two years in prison, he emerged a greater hero than before, and in 1847 was elected to the National Diet. As a delegate he could work for reforms for the people. Kossuth believed that all the people should have equality before the law regardless of

The Vienna uprising. In February 1848 a revolution broke out in France and spread quickly to Germany and the Hapsburg lands—Austria, Hungary, and Bohemia. All were put down before the end of 1849.

race, language, or religion. There should be voting, trial by jury, equal taxation. And to preserve these rights, there must be a Hungarian Constitution, a Hungarian army, and a Hungarian bank.

Such goals were beyond the imagination of the Hapsburgs. The court in Vienna organized its forces in opposition to the liberals and stirred up hatreds of the non-Hungarians in Hungary against the Hungarians. Sides were drawn and open war broke out.

The Hapsburgs were not strong enough to take control themselves. They asked the help of Russia, and Czar Nicholas I, another despot, obliged. The Hungarians had no chance to win against such odds. The Russian soldiers overwhelmed them and by October 6, 1849, their revolution was crushed.

Immediately there was a price on Kossuth's head and he fled to Turkey. While in exile he did not lose his devotion to a free Hungary and a free Europe. He expressed his deep concern in a long, fervent letter to the people of the United States, dated March 27, 1850. He explained the Hungarian motives in the Revolution, and told of the injustices imposed by the Hapsburgs. Horace Greeley published and circulated the letter. Although it was 26 pages long it was widely read.

Kossuth's popularity in the United States was so great that the American government intervened with Turkey for his freedom and officially invited him to visit the United States. On December 5, 1851, he arrived in New York on the warship *Mississippi*.

He received a hero's welcome. Witnesses said it was as enthusiastic as the receptions for Lafayette and Washington. There were cannon salutes and bands played "Yankee Doodle" and "Hail to the Chief." The mayor of New York was there with 20,000 troops to greet him officially. On the streets 100,000 people cheered and shouted.

Lajos Kossuth (1802-1894), leader of the Hungarian revolution, served as president of the independent republic of Hungary in 1849. When Russia and Austria defeated Hungarian forces, Kossuth fled to Turkey. This picture was taken during his visit to America in 1851. *(Daguerreotype courtesy of the Chicago Historical Society)*

Millard Fillmore was President of the United States at the time of Kossuth's visit. Though Secretary of State Daniel Webster sympathized with Hungary's problems, Fillmore's foreign policy did not call for intervention in the affairs of other countries.

In appearance and manner Kossuth was a memorable figure. He was pale, with brown hair and melancholy brown eyes. He had a wide beard, under the jaw and chin, and wore a high black hat with ostrich feathers. Both hat and beard became his trademarks. In prison he had taught himself the English language, using Shakespeare and the Bible as guides. His voice was rich and musical, and a tendency to use sixteenth century phrasings only added to his effectiveness.

Kossuth made each speech fit the audience. During one week in New York, he gave speeches in German, Italian, and French as well as in English. In eight months he gave some 200 speeches in the major cities of the East, the South, and the Middle West. Writers produced hundreds of pamphlets, books, and editorials about Kossuth and his ideas. A veritable "Kossuth craze" swept the country. People wore Kossuth beards and Kossuth hats. Streets, squares, cities, and counties were named after him.

But Kossuth did not wish to be only a living legend. He was a practical working statesman with serious plans in mind. Although he received approval from the populace and from many state governments, he wanted official support from the United States Government for his proposals.

To Kossuth, the defeat of Hungary by Austria involved a serious political principle. Why should one country struggling against an enemy for self-government have to take on two enemies — Russia and Austria? Kossuth felt that Hungary should get support from a fourth country, which would promise to intervene and help them. He called this the principle of "Intervention for Non-Intervention."

Secretary of State Daniel Webster gave his verbal support when he said at a banquet in January 1852:

> I limit my aspirations for Hungary for the present, to that single and simple point — Hungarian independence, Hungarian self-government, Hungarian control of Hungarian destinies.

Both Congress and President Millard Fillmore, however, could give no encouragement. Officially America was at peace with the Austrian Hapsburgs. An agreement to intervene might have meant risking war.

The Austrian ambassador in America, Chevalier Hulsemann, called Kossuth a rebel and a common criminal. American isolationists were afraid he was a war-monger, and slave-holders were uneasy about his talk of free people. Other critics considered him an extremist.

On July 14, 1852, Kossuth left the country quietly with only a small group bidding him farewell, his mission seemingly a failure. He continued his exile in England for six years and then moved to Turin, Italy, where he remained until the end of his long life.

Kossuth could have returned to Hungary if he had been willing to accept the Hapsburg rule. But he did not give way on any of his principles. To a large number of his own people he remained a spiritual leader. In a small village 180 peasants voted for him as a "write-in candidate" long after his death. In America he became a symbol for democratic methods at the time of social unrest prior to the Civil War.

His principle of Intervention for Non-Intervention was ahead of its time. It became a basic aim of the League of Nations and later of the U. N. Charter, although nations have always found decisions about intervention to be very difficult. Kossuth's excellence as an orator popularized the ideology which eventually abolished slavery in America. In fact, Abraham Lincoln may have been influenced by some of Kossuth's words, as a comparison of the following quotations suggests:

On Feb. 6, 1852, in Columbus, Ohio, Kossuth said: The spirit of our age is democracy. All for the people and all by the people. Nothing about the people without the people; that is democracy, and that is the ruling tendency of the spirit of our age . . .

On Nov. 19, 1863, at Gettysburg, Lincoln said: We here highly resolve that these dead shall not have died in vain — that this nation, under God, shall have a new birth of freedom — and that government of the people, by the people, for the people, shall not perish from the earth.

In 1958 the United States Government issued a postage stamp honoring Kossuth.

2. An International Incident

In 1853, the year after Kossuth left America, there was a citizenship problem which put another Hungarian in the news. The problem, in fact, turned into an international incident. It could have led to war. Its solution set a precedent and became a permanent part of international law. The incident again involved three countries—Austria, America, and Turkey.

The Hungarian was Martin Koszta, who had been a captain in Kossuth's army at the collapse of the Hungarian Revolution of 1848. Like Kossuth, he was a marked man and fled first to Turkey and then to America. When he arrived in America, he decided to become a citizen. He declared his intention to be naturalized, and shortly after, went on a business trip to Turkey.

While he was in Turkey he was still not a full American citizen. As a safeguard, however, he put himself under the protection of the American Consul. He also received a "safe conduct" approval from the Turks. Nevertheless, to the Austrians he was still a war criminal. They worked out a scheme to capture him.

One day while Koszta was walking along the seashore he was attacked by hired ruffians. They overpowered him and threw him into the water. He was immediately picked up by sailors waiting in a boat. The sailors delivered him to a large warship, the *Huszar*. The name *Huszar* happened to be Hungarian but the ship was Austrian. The crew put Koszta in irons.

Then the international conflict began. The Austrians said that Koszta was theirs. They said he was an Austrian subject, a "criminal traitor" who should be tried by them. The Americans said he was under their protection and demanded his release. The Austrians refused.

At that point the Americans decided to send a naval captain to get Koszta off the *Huszar*. He was Captain Duncan Nathan Ingraham, the commander of the U.S. sloop-of-war *St. Louis*, which had just arrived in port near the *Huszar*. His action to release Koszta took great courage.

President Franklin Pierce (left) and **Secretary of State William Marcy** (right) justified the American rescue of Martin Koszta from an Austrian ship. Their foreign policy was more adventurous than Fillmore's, though not always as successful as in the Koszta affair.

Ingraham first maneuvered his sloop broadside to the *Huszar*. He uncovered the sloop's guns, had the battle stations manned, and lowered a lifeboat. Then he sent an officer in full dress over to the *Huszar* to get Koszta. Again the Austrians refused. The American captain replied: "Then I am in duty bound to inform you . . . unless he is on board our ship within the next 30 minutes, we'll be compelled to take action." In less than 30 minutes Koszta was aboard the *St. Louis* and on his way to America.

The Austrians continued to protest. They said that without full citizenship Koszta was not an American, and they claimed that international law backed them up.

Americans had two answers. Secretary of State William Marcy said it was true that Koszta was not a full citizen, but that he had full legal rights. These rights, Marcy argued, were acquired "nationality rights." Koszta had been a legally admitted resident of the United States; therefore, he had full protection. Marcy also argued that Koszta was the victim of trickery and injustice, and that his release was a humanitarian action.

On these grounds the Koszta affair set a precedent. President Franklin Pierce declared that in every such case, when opportunity arose, the same principles and policy would be employed by the United States.

3. *Hungarians in the Civil War*

The names of many Hungarians are sprinkled through rosters of soldiers in the American Civil War. In 1860, on the eve of the war, there were about 4,000 Hungarians and Americans of Hungarian background living in the United States. Out of this group about 800 men volunteered for war service. While this number is not large, it was the highest ratio of volunteers to the total number achieved by any nationality group in the United States. This may be explained by the same motives that had inspired them to fight for freedom against political oppression in their native land. Many had left Hungary rather than remain humiliated subjects of the Hapsburg kings.

Many of the volunteers were ex-revolutionaries. It was natural for them to sympathize with the Northern aims of retaining the Union and emancipating the slaves. When Lincoln called for 75,000 volunteers for the Union Army on April 16, 1861, many of the Hungarian ex-revolutionaries were ready to serve.

One of the first Hungarians to volunteer was Geza Mihaloczy, who served in the Western Department, which was made up of Mississippi, Kansas, Illinois, and Kentucky. He organized a company of militia in Chicago as early as February 1861. It was called "The Lincoln Riflemen" and was composed of Hungarians and men of Bohemian and Slavonic origin. This militia merged with

General John C. Fremont (1813-1890) commanded the Western Department of the Union Army during the Civil War. Many Hungarians served under him.

the 24th Illinois Volunteer Infantry Regiment. Mihaloczy became colonel of the regiment, and served for three years before he was shot in an engagement at Buzzard Roost Gap, Tennessee. He died of his wound at Chattanooga, on March 11, 1864, and was buried there in the National Cemetery.

A relatively large group of Hungarians volunteered in the Western Department. There were special reasons for this. General John C. Fremont was the commanding officer. Fremont was an inspiring leader and the Hungarians were attracted to him. More important, they also wanted to serve in positions which equaled their capacities. Just as in the Revolutionary War, the employment of "foreigners" in leading positions in the Army was strongly discouraged. In the Western Department, however, there was a great need for more men and officers, a demand which could be met in only a limited way by West Point. Fremont had no choice but to employ "foreigners."

Among many Hungarians who served with Fremont was Brigadier General Alexander Asboth, chief-of-staff. He had been a colonel of Engineers in the Hungarian Revolution and came to the United States with Kossuth on the American man-of-war *Mississippi*. Asboth distinguished himself in the battle of Pea Ridge, Arkansas, where he was wounded in the left arm. Despite his

Brigadier General Alexander Asboth (1811-1868)

Major Charles Zagonyi in dress uniform. The negative of Mathew Brady's photograph has deteriorated in the years since the Civil War.

wound he was in the saddle the next morning. In the Marianna engagement in Florida his left arm was shattered by a bullet, and another bullet became lodged under his right cheekbone. He survived, and after the war was appointed U.S. Minister to the Argentine Republic, where he died in 1868.

Another remarkable Hungarian staff officer in Fremont's Western Department was Major Charles Zagonyi. He had been a hussar officer in the Hungarian war for independence. In America his applications to be an officer were rejected in the East, so he traveled west to Fremont, who commissioned him to organize his cavalry guard. Within a few days Zagonyi organized the first company, which became known as Fremont's Body Guard. As an expert horseman he put together three more companies of local trappers, hunters, and pioneers in rapid succession and was appointed the Commander of the Body Guard.

He owes his fame to a hussar dash on the enemy which became known as the Zagonyi death-ride. The Confederates held a strategic hill near the town of Springfield, Missouri. Fremont believed that the enemy numbered only about 300 men and appointed Zagonyi to attack them with a corresponding force. However, just before the attack, scouts reported that the enemy numbered close to 2,000 men. Fremont decided to delay the action until more troops could arrive.

Zagonyi, however, did not want to call off the attack since his men were ready to fight. He explained the situation to his soldiers and told those who did not want to fight to step back. "Not a man flinched."

The cavalry attacked the hill and the enemy was completely routed. Fremont compared this deed with the famous Charge of the Light Brigade at the Battle of Balaklava in the Crimean War.

Hungarians did fight on the Eastern front. The Garibaldi Guard of New York was part of the 39th New York Infantry Regiment and had a large Hungarian-born contingent. About half of the men came from Hungary, and the Hungarian George Utassy was their first colonel.

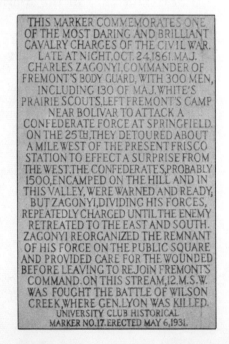

THIS MARKER COMMEMORATES ONE OF THE MOST DARING AND BRILLIANT CAVALRY CHARGES OF THE CIVIL WAR. LATE AT NIGHT, OCT. 24,1861, MAJ. CHARLES ZAGONYI, COMMANDER OF FREMONT'S BODY GUARD, WITH 300 MEN, INCLUDING 130 OF MAJ. WHITE'S PRAIRIE SCOUTS, LEFT FREMONT'S CAMP NEAR BOLIVAR TO ATTACK A CONFEDERATE FORCE AT SPRINGFIELD. ON THE 25TH, THEY DETOURED ABOUT A MILE WEST OF THE PRESENT FRISCO STATION TO EFFECT A SURPRISE FROM THE WEST. THE CONFEDERATES, PROBABLY 1500, ENCAMPED ON THE HILL AND IN THIS VALLEY, WERE WARNED AND READY, BUT ZAGONYI, DIVIDING HIS FORCES, REPEATEDLY CHARGED UNTIL THE ENEMY RETREATED TO THE EAST AND SOUTH. ZAGONYI REORGANIZED THE REMNANT OF HIS FORCE ON THE PUBLIC SQUARE AND PROVIDED CARE FOR THE WOUNDED BEFORE LEAVING TO REJOIN FREMONT'S COMMAND. ON THIS STREAM, 12. M.S.W. WAS FOUGHT THE BATTLE OF WILSON CREEK, WHERE GEN. LYON WAS KILLED. UNIVERSITY CLUB HISTORICAL MARKER NO. 17. ERECTED MAY 6, 1931.

A granite monument in Springfield, Missouri, honors Zagonyi's cavalry charge upon Confederate forces in October 1861.

General Julius Stahel (1825-1912)

One of the Hungarians on the Eastern front, Julius H. Stahel, became a general and had a highly distinguished military career. In Hungary Stahel had been a bookseller and a first lieutenant in the war for independence. In America he was a journalist until the Civil War gave him a chance to make better use of his talent.

In the first Battle of Bull Run, Stahel covered the retreating Union Army with his 8th New York Infantry Regiment, an action which prevented the Confederate Army from advancing on Washington. In 1863 Stahel was appointed to the post of Commander of the 11th Army Corps, but the post went to Carl Schurz, the leader of German-Americans. Stahel yielded the command to Schurz because of his friendship for him.

Stahel also distinguished himself at the battle of Piedmont, Virginia. While wounded, he personally led a cavalry charge which decided the battle in favor of the Union Army. For his bravery he received the Congressional Medal of Honor.

Among the 800 Hungarian volunteers in the Union Army about 100 were officers. The Hungarians' libertarian spirit and military skill were recognized by the United States Government. Several of the outstanding leaders were given honoring medals and diplomatic assignment in foreign countries.

PART III

Tidal Waves of Immigration

1. *Hope on the Horizon*

Like the Hungarian ex-revolutionaries, other Europeans in the nineteenth century came to America to be free of political persecution. They came also to find better work, land, and homes. At the end of the eighteenth century and during the first half of the nineteenth, Europe was in a state of political shambles and economic degradation. The French Revolution and the Napoleonic wars took their toll. Poverty and hunger started a large-scale exodus of people from Europe to a better life in America.

Emigration to America was more readily considered by men whose countries touched the sea. The first immigrants to America came from an area with plenty of seashore — the British Isles and western Europe. This, of course, did not include Hungary, a land-locked country without a seashore.

2. *First Wave of Immigration, 1890-1910*

During the first half of the nineteenth century, most immigrants came from northern Europe — Great Britain, Ireland, Germany, and the Scandinavian countries. In the second half of the century although Scandinavian emigration increased, the proportion from western Europe rapidly declined. From 1890 to 1910 less than one-third came from these countries; the bulk of the rest came from Central and Eastern Europe, including Hungary.

3. *Immigrants from the Land of Hungary*

American statistics consider every immigrant born within the borders of historical Hungary a Hungarian. However, not all people from within these borders have considered themselves Hungarian, since the borderlines changed two or even three times

Arpad, a Magyar chieftain, led his tribe into the plain of the Danube River in about 895 A.D. His descendants — first chieftains and then kings — ruled Hungary until 1301. A statue of Arpad stands in Budapest.

within a generation. The changes were due to wars and peace treaties. These treaties were made at negotiating tables, with little concern for the people who were primarily affected by them.

Thus, many immigrants from the land of Hungary considered themselves German, Croat, Serbian, Rumanian, or Slovak, depending mainly on their original tongue. Why did Hungary include groups of people with such different backgrounds? The answer is not simple; it lies in the turmoil of more than 1,000 years of history. A brief review can help illuminate the events that created polyglot areas in the Carpathian Basin.

4. *Border Changes and Hungarian History*

The first border was staked out when seven nomadic Hungarian tribes occupied the area in the ninth century. Under one leader, Arpad, they made a "blood" alliance to protect each other against other migrating tribes, and vowed to keep and develop the land for themselves. Assuming Christianity, within about two centuries they developed a life comparable to other kingdoms of the Middle Ages.

A delegation of electors proclaims **Matthias Corvinus** (1443-1490) king of Hungary, 1458. Aided by a large standing army, Matthias fought the Turks and conquered his neighbors to the north and east. In Hungary, he administered justice with impartial firmness, supported the arts and sciences, and established a fine library.

Then in 1241 the first alien force invaded. They were the Tartars; their leader was Batu Khan. They remained for one year, and killed half the population, including women and children. They ravaged, pillaged, and burnt the Hungarian Kingdom. The country was so depleted that immigration into Hungary became necessary. Many Germans came in, settled, and helped to rebuild the country. By the time of Matthias Corvinus, a great and memorable king who reigned between 1458 and 1490, Hungary had become a powerful, creative, dynamic state. Cultural life, comfort, and power were comparable to that of England in the late fifteenth century.

The golden age of Matthias disappeared as the Ottoman Turkish invaders gradually took over. Their victory at the battle of Mohacs in 1526 marked the start of 150 years of Turkish domination. The Turks split up the country, leaving but a narrow portion of the Carpathian Basin for the Hungarians to control. The Turks ruled till the 1690's when they were turned back from Vienna. They left the country with a drastically reduced, impoverished, and hungry population.

·SVLEYMAN·IMPERATORTVR·

Oē grooté turc keyser vā cōstant

Suleiman I (1494-1566) became sultan of the Ottoman Empire in 1520. Under Suleiman the Turks made their greatest gains in power and territory. In August 1526 he defeated Louis II's Hungarian forces in the battle of Mohacs.

The struggle with the Turks affected all of Europe, and lasted some 400 years—longer than the actual Turkish occupation of Hungary. It was a long drawn-out war demanding fighting soldiers and their lives. It also meant that the Hapsburgs from Austria, who helped in the final defeat of the Turks in Hungary, gained more and more control over Hungary. They invited fugitives and refugees from neighboring lands to repopulate Hungary, where they could live in relative safety.

Louis II (1506-1526) became king of Hungary at the age of 10. Life in his court was one party after another, while finances dwindled and the army went hungry. At Mohacs, Louis and most of his 20,000 men were killed by an army of 80,000 Turks. Weighed down by his armor, Louis sank into a bog and drowned.

33

Hungarian dragoon of the sixteenth century.

5. *Non-Hungarians in Hungary*

This pattern of wars and devastation, building and rebuilding recurred throughout Hungarian history. Hungarians learned to accept a wide variety of groups in their midst. Germans, French, Italians, Cumans, Petcheneggs, Slovaks, Serbs, Croats, Rumanians, Ruthenians, Poles, Jews, Armenians, and Turks all found a livelihood within the borders of Hungary.

By the time of the mass emigration to America, several of these non-Hungarian nationalities were absorbed into Hungary but many of them maintained their separate identities. In some villages people could speak two or even three different languages. Some of these languages were close to each other, and sometimes members of two different groups, each speaking his own tongue, were able to communicate.

Many times, however, differences existed beyond the language. The backgrounds of the three basic groups, Ural-Altaic (Hungarian), German, and Slavic, reflected deep-rooted differences. In addition to language, they had different historical backgrounds, occupations, religions, and traditions.

Despite this the people themselves were able to get along and live in relative harmony, especially on a "food and shelter" basis. Common dangers emphasized the need for unity, but disagreements were actually encouraged by those in power. Kings and emperors emphasized their differences and stirred up one group against another. The people became the emperor's prey. Such an atmosphere was frustrating enough to cause emigration from the land of Hungary.

6. *Other Reasons for Immigration*

The greatest frustration of all, however, was not political but economic. The status of the commoner — the serf, the peasant, the industrial worker — was miserable no matter what language he spoke. He faced possible starvation. If he could own a piece of land in his own village he might stave off hunger. But how could he save enough money to buy a piece of land? The answer lay in America. Seeking financial improvement was a powerful motivation to emigrate. Many left intending to return to their native villages to buy a desired piece of land.

Hungarian farm workers gather and shock wheat. For centuries wealthy landlords owned most of the land, which was farmed by peasants. To escape poverty, many emigrated to America in the late nineteenth century.

A group of immigrants from Central and Eastern Europe arrive at Ellis Island, 1900. The peak year for Hungarian immigration was 1907.

7. *The Newcomer's Life in America*

When a peasant or industrial worker arrived in America he usually contacted someone he already knew from his native village or a neighboring village. His friend was able to arrange a job for him in a factory, sweatshop, or mine. He did not speak English but he did not really need to. He could even buy newspapers printed in his native language.

And in heavily Hungarian areas he could even use his native Hungarian for shopping. There were large Hungarian settlements in New York, Pittsburgh, Cleveland, Dayton, and Youngstown, and in many of the larger towns in New York, Pennsylvania, West Virginia, Ohio, and Illinois. In his Hungarian church—Catholic, Protestant, or Jewish—he could worship in his native tongue. If he became sick or died, the Hungarian insurance company took care of him.

And he could find his own social life, with a chance for marriage. At the picnics of the church or insurance company he met his future wife, perhaps a pretty Hungarian girl who may have come from the same village. When their first child arrived he bought a house and decided to make more money to care for his family. By the time his first child left school, the house was paid for; and the parents had decided to stay in America and see the rest of their children through school. Eventually their own children no longer spoke Hungarian regularly. Some of them shunned all of their Hungarian connections and, sadly enough, even their parents.

8. *Statistics on Immigration*

How many Hungarians came to America in the first wave of immigration? It is difficult to arrive at an exact figure. The three possible sources for this figure are: the Immigration and Naturalization Service, the Hungarian pre-World War I emigration figures, and the figures of European ports of embarkation. The figures are not all in agreement, and they are sometimes incomplete.

According to the U.S. Census figures, it is fair to say that between 1871 and 1913 a total of 1,893,647 immigrants arrived in the United States from the land of Hungary. The peak of arrival was reached in 1907 when 193,460 of the year's total of 1,285,439 arrived from Hungary. These figures include Slovaks, Serbians, Rumanians, Croats, Ruthenians, and perhaps others. All of these immigrants were born within the borders of Hungary, but might have chosen to be called by the nationality of their language.

Occupations of immigrants in the first wave are suggested by the following percentages, from 1907:

Farmhands and farmers	67.0%
Unskilled workers	12.5%
Factory hands and miners	12.4%
Domestic servants	5.5%
Misc. group, out of which 0.5% were professional	2.6%

Percentages of the Hungarian and non-Hungarian groups from Hungary who emigrated at this peak period can be estimated in a very general way by looking at the distribution of nationalities within Hungary in 1910. The proportion is as follows:

Hungarians	55.0%
Rumanians	16.0%
Germans	10.5%
Slovaks	10.5%
Ruthenians	2.5%
Serbs	2.5%
Others	3.0%

The breakdown of United States immigration figures into male and female shows an interesting irregularity when compared with the Hungarian emigration figures. Many males were apparently "bootlegged" into the United States, so that they would not be caught at the point of embarkation. If they were of draft age, as a large number of them were, they could not have emigrated. They would have been held back and drafted into the Austrian army.

Whatever the occupation or national background of these immigrants, most of them had in their formative years a Hungarian education. They contributed their diligence and courage to the development of American industries, making good use of the opportunity provided for them in the United States.

PART IV

Age of the
Professional Immigrant

The long period of mass migration lasted up to the eve of World War I. During and after the war it changed considerably, both in numbers and background of the immigrants. The age of mass migration became the age of the professional immigrant. There are a number of important reasons for this change.

After the war the relationship between America and Europe changed. Prosperous European countries which had been creditors to the United States became debtors after 1918. While four years of war had exhausted the economic reserves of the continent, American industry was spurred on by the European war market.

There was little immigration during the war. There were no ships available to transport men, and Europe needed working hands and fighting soldiers. In the postwar years, however, America again became a desirable refuge, and immigration picked up rapidly.

Many Americans became alarmed. They feared competition for jobs, and changes in familiar social patterns. Responding to their fears and prejudices, Congress devised a system of restrictions to keep away large masses of unskilled laborers. Quotas were spelled out in several acts during the years between 1921 and 1929. This marked the end of the age of mass migration.

The quotas revealed apparent favoritism. They tended to reduce the inflow of people from Central Europe in preference to those from Western Europe. This meant that entry by Hungarian workers and farmers was drastically cut. The laws made it possible for a few Hungarians to emigrate, especially professionals.

1. *Hungary After World War I*

In 1867 Hungary and Austria, after years of struggle, had reached a compromise. They joined to form the Austro-Hungarian Empire, or Dual Monarchy. Hungary attained self-government except in questions of foreign affairs, finance, and war. These areas of government were shared with Austria. They also shared a ruler; the emperor of Austria would henceforth be king of Hungary too.

As part of the Austro-Hungarian Empire, Hungary was allied with Germany in World War I. At the end of the lost war the function of government almost ceased. The economy, which had prospered before 1914, faded away, producing a climate of lawlessness, unemployment, poverty, and political unrest.

Franz Joseph I (1830-1916) became emperor of Austria in December 1848, when his uncle Ferdinand gave up the throne during the revolution. In 1867 the Dual Monarchy was formed and Franz Joseph received the Hungarian crown as well. The murder of his heir, Franz Ferdinand, in June 1914, started a chain of events leading to the outbreak of World War I.

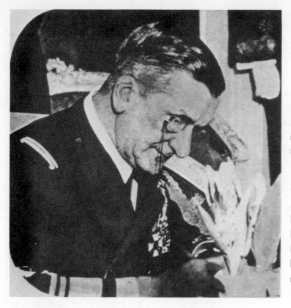

Admiral Nicholas Horthy de Nagybanya (1868-1957) commanded the Austro-Hungarian navy during World War I and became Regent of Hungary in 1920. After his forced resignation in 1944, the Germans shipped him to a castle in Bavaria where American troops later found and released him. Horthy testified at the Nuremberg trials of 1946 but he was not charged with war crimes. In 1949 he retired to Portugal.

These conditions reached the proportion of a revolution, forcing the king, Charles IV, to resign. The Dual Monarchy collapsed in November 1918 and a socialist government was proclaimed. It was called The Hungarian Republic. Its president, Michael Karolyi, took office in January 1919. His inexperienced cabinet could not cope with the country's problems, and in March he ceded his power to the communist government of Bela Kun.

His rule was also brief. After a few months of government by terror—known as the "red terror"—the people of Hungary turned against his regime. When Bela Kun's forces were defeated by invading Rumanians in August 1919, he fled the country, leaving it in a state of anarchy. In the absence of a formal government a reaction to the red terror developed. These reprisals became known as the "white terror." Within a few months anti-communist groups were able to form a government, with Admiral Horthy de Nagybanya as their leader. Horthy entered Budapest with his troops in November 1919, shortly after the Rumanians had left. He became Regent of Hungary in 1920 and held this position until 1944, although most of the actual governing was handled by a series of premiers.

HUNGARY IN 1914

Hungary's settlement with the Allies after World War I was signed in the Grand Trianon Palace at Versailles, France, in 1920. The treaty gave portions of Hungary to Rumania and to the newly formed nations of Yugoslavia and Czechoslovakia. These areas of mixed population had long been trouble spots in the sprawling Hapsburg empire. Hungary recovered some of her land before and during World War II, but a postwar treaty restored the Trianon boundaries.

HUNGARY TODAY

The new regime had to deal with severe losses dictated by the peace treaty of Trianon (1920). The terms of the treaty were considered unfair by most Hungarians. Hungary lost two-thirds of its prewar area and 60% of its original population. At least 3.2 million Hungarians lived outside the new borders of Hungary. The loss in land and resources was staggering. She lost 61% of her arable land, 88% of her timber, and 56% of her industrial plants. The new government attempted land reforms but could not deal effectively with the problem. Hard feelings persisted between peasants and landowners, workers and industrialists. The low American quota prevented peasants and workers from emigrating. Before 1914 they could leave Hungary if they had no other solution to the problem of poverty.

Education in Hungary before the war emphasized high attainment, and created an excess of professionals. With the United States quota system also favoring professionals, it was the time for doctors, scientists, engineers, artists, and white-collar workers to leave the impoverished country and find a better life.

Many of these immigrants were of Jewish origin. For some of them life had become politically difficult in Hungary during the 1920's. In the early part of the twentieth century, Jews had become active in socialist movements throughout Europe. In Hungary, in the aftermath of World War I, they had a leading role in the regimes of Karolyi and Kun. After the failure of these regimes, anti-Semitic feelings ran high. Much of this was demonstrated in white terror activities directed against the Jews, even those who had no connection with the earlier red terror.

This was in strong contrast with their position in the second part of the nineteenth century. At that time, Hungary was considered a haven for Jewish immigrants, primarily from Russia and Rumania, where they were persecuted. They became tradesmen, bankers, industrialists, and landowners in the developing economy of Hungary. Many married into the aristocracy and occupied important positions as judges, educators, and government officials. The economic problems of Hungary, as well as the anti-Semitism after World War I, played a part in the decision of many Hungarian Jews, largely professionals, to emigrate.

The professionals' life in America differed from the life of the immigrants who came before World War I. The earlier immigrants settled in the Hungarian ghettos of American cities. There they could manage to live without knowing the English language. The professionals, on the other hand, picked up English rapidly and were quickly integrated into American intellectual life.

Immigrant Aliens Admitted to the United States from Hungary, 1935-1965

1935-1939	3,702	1953	803
1940	1,902	1954	1,163
1941	886	1955	904
1942	284	1956	2,261
1943	163	1957	8,705
1944	212	1958	1,583
1945	117	1959	30,098
1946	577	1960	7,257
1947	1,277	1961	1,466
1948	1,471	1962	1,355
1949	1,998	1963	1,766
1950	5,098	1964	1,813
1951	4,922	1965	1,574
1952	6,850		

In statistics, it is somewhat difficult to pinpoint the exact number of professionals who emigrated. Within the four years following the war about 25,000 Hungarians came to the United States. The 1921 Emergency Quota Act permitted the immigration of 5,747 persons of Hungarian birth every year. The 1929 Act reduced this number to 869. In the depression the figure was the lowest, at 284. With World War II approaching and the number of political refugees rising, the yearly figure of immigrants from Hungary increased to 1,348 in 1939 and 1,902 in 1940.

A bombed-out office building, Budapest, 1945. About 70% of the city was destroyed or badly damaged during the war.

2. *World War II*

Between the two World Wars, political and economic developments in Germany and Soviet Russia (including the rise of nazism in one and communism in the other) left little margin of choice to a small country located between the larger powers. Hoping for German support to regain some of her lost land, Hungary in the 1930's approached a somewhat reluctant alliance with Nazi Germany.

Hungarian Jews enter a freight train bound for a German concentration camp, 1944. About half of Hungary's 800,000 Jews were deported, most of them to the largest and nearest of the death camps—Auschwitz, in southern Poland. (Photograph courtesy YIVO Institute for Jewish Research)

Hungary entered the war in June 1941, joining Germany in the invasion of Russia. Hungarian forces were badly defeated during the retreat from Russia, and Hungary's active part in the war was very limited from 1943 on. In March 1944 the Germans invaded and occupied Hungary. As the Russians approached, in October 1944, Horthy tried to make a separate peace, but the Germans made him withdraw his proclamation. They forced him to resign and installed a puppet government of Hungarian Nazis. Russian forces took Budapest and defeated the German army. In January 1945 the Provisional National Government of Occupied Hungary signed an armistice with the Allies.

The war displaced a large number of Hungarians. Many of Jewish background felt lucky if they were able to evade Nazi persecution by hiding or fleeing abroad. During the Nazi occupation about 450,000 of Hungary's 800,000 Jews were taken from Hungary and sent to concentration camps. Adolph Eichmann organized the deportations in the spring and early summer of 1944, and was aided by pro-Nazi members of the Hungarian government. For several years Horthy had resisted the extreme measures demanded by the Germans. In the summer of 1944 he refused to yield Budapest's 200,000 Jews to the Nazis, but after his downfall over 30,000 of them were deported. Later the occupying Russian army found 124,000 Jews in the city of Budapest.

During the Russian advance upon Hungary, many Hungarians who remembered the 1919 communist terror chose to flee westward. Eventually about 30,000 of those Hungarians who survived the concentration camps and hostilities fled the country and reached the United States between 1945 and 1955 as displaced persons.

3. *Hungary After World War II*

After the war, Russia retained control of the Eastern European countries which she had conquered from the Germans. In the Hungarian election of 1947, the middle-of-the-road Small Landholders party received 56% of the vote and the Communists only 17%. But the Communist leader, Matyas Rakosi (supported by Russian forces occupying Hungary), dominated the coalition government of Ferenc Nagy. In 1948, when Marshal Tito of Yugoslavia broke with Russia, Rakosi feared that the same thing might happen in Hungary. He put an end to the coalition, and the Communist party gained full control.

Under Rakosi, Hungary was molded more and more closely on the Soviet pattern. Free speech and individual liberties were sharply curtailed. Many people were imprisoned without reason, and the secret police (AVH) caused a large part of the population to live in fear.

Economic recovery in the decade after the war was slow and difficult, and national planning often incompetent. The war had destroyed two-thirds of the animal stock and about one-half of the useful living quarters in Hungary. The support of occupation forces and Soviet removals were a further drain upon the economy. In addition, the Soviet Union demanded the payment of postwar reparations as a result of Hungary's invasion of Russia. American officials at the time felt that the reparation costs were out of proportion to Hungary's part in the war and to her ability to pay.

Travel in the postwar decade was severely restricted. When the western borders were sealed with barbed wire, minefields, and watch towers, emigration from Hungary became almost impossible.

Rebels surround the bodies of AVH members. The secret police were
shot as they came out of their headquarters in Budapest, October 1956.

4. *The 1956 Revolution and Its Refugees*

By 1956 the harshness of Soviet control diminished somewhat.
Joseph Stalin had died in 1953, and under the relative liberalization
of Nikita Khrushchev several Eastern European countries took
steps toward greater freedom. The Hungarian Revolution of 1956
was unlike most revolutions because it had little planning, and no
leaders at the outset. It was a spontaneous explosion, and attempts
to quell it only increased the rage of the population.

At the beginning of the revolution the leading role was played
by articulate Hungarian Communist intellectuals whose forebears
were the Hungarian freedom fighters of 1848. On the night of
October 22, 1956, a group of university students put forth 16 demands, similar to parts of the American Bill of Rights and the Charter of the United Nations. With peaceful demonstrators from all
walks of life—workers, soldiers, old people—they marched to
the Radio Building in Budapest to broadcast their demands.

The secret police who guarded the building opened fire on the
demonstrators, and two weeks of fighting began. Workers, students,
women, and children, often aided by Hungarian soldiers, fought
against the much-hated AVH and later against Russian tanks.

A short-lived free regime was headed by Imre Nagy, a Communist himself (and premier from 1953 to 1955). Nagy separated Hungary from the Warsaw Treaty, thus cutting its military ties with the Communist bloc. He declared Hungary neutral, and contacted the United Nations by radio, explaining the Soviet intention to take military control of the country. Neither the United States nor the United Nations, preoccupied with a crisis in the Middle East over the Suez Canal, provided any decisive political action against the Soviets. An overwhelming Russian military force overran the capital on November 3, and after about a week of fighting the revolution was subdued.

Repression followed. The freedom fighters were tried in criminal courts; many were convicted and executed, including Imre Nagy in 1958. Many of the younger fighters were kept in jail to stand trial when they reached the age of 18; several of them were executed. About 200,000 people sought refuge in Western Europe. Out of the 200,000 about 30,000, primarily young men — the freedom fighters — reached the United States to start a new life.

A Hungarian family in Vienna, en route to the United States. They escaped from Budapest after the revolution of 1956.

The entire world watched the developments in Hungary with sympathy. In 1957 *Time* magazine made the Hungarian freedom fighter Man of the Year, honoring him for his moral courage. Books of all kinds were inspired by the revolution: biographical descriptions of events, philosophical essays, rewritings of military strategy, novels, poems, and films.

States with over 10,000 People of Hungarian Stock, 1960 Census

New York	142,834
Ohio	100,786
Pennsylvania	83,417
New Jersey	82,017
Michigan	46,811
Illinois	43,005
Connecticut	25,367
Indiana	17,983
Florida	17,229
Wisconsin	14,982

For Census purposes, people are of foreign stock if they were born abroad or have at least one parent born abroad. In 1960 Mississippi had the fewest people of Hungarian stock — 217.

During the 1960's travel restrictions in Hungary have been eased, both for Hungarians and for tourists from the West. American film makers have found that Budapest provides an excellent location for films which take place anywhere in turn-of-the century Europe. MGM's film *The Fixer* was shot in and around Budapest, with an American-English cast, Hungarian crew and equipment, and Hungarian extras. Above, American director John Frankenheimer is seated next to an old Hungarian women who appears in the film. Below, Frankenheimer with the crew.

PART V

Prominent Hungarians in America

America has profited from the pursuit of excellence in Hungarian culture. The so-called "brain drain" has contributed a large number of expertly trained, highly educated Hungarians to America. Many have become prominent in their fields and some have become internationally known.

1. *Scientists*

Hungary before the first World War was a favorable place for the development of scientific life. A relatively prosperous economy called for progress in academic fields. As the country became more industrialized, the government encouraged and supported the building of railroads, roads, bridges, and flood control works. Technology and science progressed together.

At the same time, Hungarians heard about bold industrial adventures in America, which became an irresistible attraction to men who believed in adventures, especially those of the mind. This attraction grew as the shadow of World War II approached.

Theodore von Karman (1881-1963) was an aeronautical engineer who became a pioneer in the field of aviation. His work provided basic and widely used theories on the structure of aircraft and in aerodynamics. His ideas influenced the designs of the Bell XI, the first airplane to break the sound barrier.

Theodore von Karman (1881-1963), aeronautical engineer, taught at California Institute of Technology from 1930 until 1949. His autobiography, *The Wind and Beyond*, was published in 1967.

Von Karman was raised in an academic atmosphere in Budapest where his father was a law professor at the University. Although law was considered one of the highest pursuits, he followed his own interest in the physical sciences. He received a degree in engineering at the Hungarian Royal Technical University and after graduation worked in a machine-manufacturing company where he was able to apply some of the theories he had learned. He then studied for his doctorate in Germany, and taught there.

During World War I von Karman returned to Hungary to head the research department of the Austrian-Hungarian Aviation Corps. Back in Germany after the war he directed the Aeronautical Institute at the University of Aachen. By this time his work was becoming known around the world and he was asked to lecture in various cities, including many in America. In 1928 von Karman came to the United States, where he spent the rest of his life.

He became director of the Guggenheim Aeronautics Laboratory at the California Institute of Technology, and in 1944 was appointed chairman of the Advisory Board of the U.S. Army Air Forces. After 1952 he served as chairman of the NATO advisory group for Aeronautical Research and Development.

Scientists of the world honored him for his capacity to describe and interpret complicated phenomena in clear, relatively simple terms. His interest covered a rather wide range within the physical sciences: physics, engineering, applied mathematics, aerodynamics, and hydrodynamics. In 1954 von Karman received the Wright Brothers Memorial Trophy for outstanding achievement and contribution to the field of aeronautics.

The Hungarian-born mathematician, John von Neumann (1903-1957), was widely respected by his fellow mathematicians. After his studies in Budapest he became an assistant professor of mathematics at Berlin University and, at the age of 28, professor of mathematics and physics at Princeton University.

His "theory of games" systematizes the chances in games using terms well known in mathematics — methods which some critics feel may also be applied to such subjects as political science and military strategy. Von Neumann, whose work was important in the development of missiles and electronic computers, was a winner of the Fermi Award and a member of the Atomic Energy Commission.

John von Neumann (1903-1957) developed the mathematical theory of games. In 1933 he became one of the first members of the Institute for Advanced Study at Princeton, New Jersey.

Nuclear physicists **Edward Teller** (left), professor at the University of California, and **Eugene Wigner** (right) of Princeton University. Teller's work led to development of the hydrogen bomb. Both men have been members of the Atomic Energy Commission and have received Fermi Awards.

Three Hungarian-born scientists have been vitally involved in the field of atomic energy. Leo Szilard, Eugene Wigner, and Edward Teller were among the physicists, American and foreign-born, who worked with Enrico Fermi to produce the first nuclear chain reaction (1942) and subsequently, the atomic bomb. In 1939 Szilard and Wigner had suggested that Albert Einstein write a letter to President Roosevelt, urging the United States Government to support the development of atomic energy. Fearing German development of an atomic bomb, scientists in the United States began secret research in about 1940. In this effort the Hungarian physicists took a considerable part.

Leo Szilard (1898-1964). With Enrico Fermi, Szilard developed the arrangement of bauxite and uranium which became the first nuclear chain reactor. He later worked tirelessly to prevent the harmful use of atomic energy and to educate the public on problems of fallout and nuclear arms control. Szilard and Wigner shared the Atoms for Peace award in 1963.

With the bomb's creation came the moral question of its use. It did not leave untouched the atomic physicists themselves, who had produced the monster. Szilard, Teller, and Wigner took part in the controversy with the others. How should it be used? Should it be used at all? Their answers were at wide variance. The United States Government decided that the security of America should be placed ahead of the moral suggestions.

All three of the Hungarian physicists have received a number of notable awards. Eugene Wigner was singled out in 1963 for the Nobel Prize in Physics.

Two other Hungarian Nobel Prize winners are Albert Szent-Gyorgyi and Gyorgy von Bekesy. Szent-Gyorgyi is best known for his research on Vitamin C. He received the Nobel Prize for Medicine and Physiology in 1937. Von Bekesy received the prize in 1961, for his studies of the inner ear.

Albert Szent-Gyorgyi (left) isolated and identified vitamin C which he extracted in large quantities from Hungarian paprika. He has directed the Institute for Muscle Research at Woods Hole, Massachusetts, since 1947 when he came to the United States. **Gyorgy von Bekesy** (right), a biophysicist, works at Harvard University.

Bela Bartok (1881-1945), composer and collector of folk music, was also a noted pianist and teacher. He toured the United States in concert during the late 1920's and settled in New York in 1940.

2. *Musicians*

The world of music is filled with Hungarian names — opera singers, instrumentalists, composers, conductors. Many of these are prominent Hungarian-Americans.

Music is an essential part of Hungarian life. The Hungarians also value music as a vocation, for it is the language which communicates feelings far beyond the capacity of everyday words. A nation's folk music, especially, springs directly from the mood and the life of the people.

Hungarian folk music is very rich and expressive. Love songs, children's play songs, tunes for birth and death became a source for the classical music of two great Hungarian musicians, Bela Bartok and Zoltan Kodaly. Of the two, Bartok (1881-1945) became in his later years a Hungarian in America. He came to this country in 1940 to avoid living under the Nazi harassment. A Dutch critic called Bartok "the most perfect musician of our age. As a man he was as marvelous as the compositions he produced."

As an accomplished musician in Budapest, Bartok happened to hear authentic folk songs sung by servant girls working in the city. The songs struck him as unusually pure and clear, and he wanted to hear more. He traveled into the remote areas of Hungary and embarked on an ambitious program of collecting as many folk songs as possible. Using an Edison phonograph with wax cylinders, he coaxed hundreds of country people to help him record them. Then he painstakingly transcribed and codified the songs they sang for him.

In his rural travels, Bartok became very attached to the simple earthbound way of life. Throughout his life, he instinctively loved everything that was real and natural. His collection of folk songs revealed conclusively that they were of purer quality than the popular gypsy songs, many of which were made up by city composers.

His enthusiasm for collecting carried him beyond the borders of Hungary. He went in 1913 as far as Algeria in North Africa to live among the nomads of Biskra, having first learned their language. He also collected Rumanian, Slovak, and Turkish folk songs.

Through this dedicated work Bartok was convinced that national jealousies are senseless and can only bring misery. He felt that folksong interchange was a medium for friendship the world over, and promoted the idea of both scientific and artistic cooperation among collectors.

His collecting resulted in the publication of 12 volumes, which included 2,700 Hungarian songs, 3,500 Hungarian-Rumanian songs, and several hundred Turkish and Arabic songs. He developed a method of collecting songs, a systematic approach worked out through the years. This method was useful for song collectors in any country.

Song-collecting for Bartok was not only an academic exercise. The songs became a part of him and a part of his work. He found them an endless source of original melody and musical vitality, and drew from them in his classical compositions. Though "modern," his works are an established part of the concert world today.

Antal Dorati, conductor of the Stockholm Philharmonic Orchestra. Dorati directed the Minneapolis Symphony Orchestra from 1949 until 1960, and has been a guest conductor of orchestras throughout Europe.

His music is frequently dissonant and uses a wide variety of scale and rhythm; it is vigorous and emotionally intense.

In America, though Bartok was ill, he continued to compose until his death in New York City in 1945.

A musician who helped promote the music of Bartok and Kodaly was a Hungarian, Ernst von Dohnanyi (1877-1960), who settled in the United States in 1949. He was a teacher at Florida State College and was also a conductor and a pianist. One of his compositions, "Ruralia Hungaria" (1926), honors his native land; another honors his adopted land—"American Rhapsody" (1954).

Another link with the musical world of Bartok and Kodaly is the well-known conductor, Antal Dorati. He studied with both of these men in his student years in Budapest. Dorati made his American debut in 1937 with the National Symphony Orchestra in Washington, and later distinguished himself as conductor of the Dallas Symphony Orchestra and the Minneapolis Symphony Orchestra.

Hungarian-Americans conduct over 30 of the some 500 orchestras in the United States. They have conducted major orchestras in three cities: Fritz Reiner was Conductor of the Chicago Philharmonic, George Szell is Music Director of the Cleveland Orchestra, and Eugene Ormandy is Conductor and Music Director of the Philadelphia Orchestra. All three spent their formative years in Hungary, showed talent at an early age, and became great conductors in America.

George Szell conducted in Berlin, Prague, and Glasgow during the 1920's and 1930's. He worked at the Metropolitan Opera in New York before joining the Cleveland Orchestra in 1946.

One of the most famous instrumentalists of Hungarian background in America is Joseph Szigeti, a virtuoso violinist. He has appeared with all the major orchestras in America, and critics have called him a "musician's musician."

A Hungarian dancer, Lorand Andahazy, has greatly enriched ballet in the Middle West with his original company, the Andahazy Ballet Borealis. Andahazy and his wife, Anna Adrianova, head one of the few American companies fully prepared to perform complete traditional ballets. The company's studio is in Edina, Minnesota, a suburb of Minneapolis, where the Andahazys also conduct a school of classical ballet.

Eugene Ormandy has conducted the Philadelphia Orchestra since 1936, longer than any other living conductor of a major orchestra. He directed the Minneapolis Symphony Orchestra from 1932 to 1936.

Joseph Pulitzer (1847-1911)

3. *Journalism*

Success stories of the immigrant boy who made a name for himself have recurred throughout American history. One of these stories is that of Joseph Pulitzer, a Hungarian of amazing zeal and resourcefulness. At the turn of the century, he made his work and his name important in the world of journalism.

His early years were spent in Mako, Hungary, where his father was a prosperous grain and onion merchant. When bankruptcy forced him out of business, he took his family to Budapest to try his luck in other trades, but his health failed and he died. His wife married another tradesman whose work meant little to his 15-year old stepson. Joseph Pulitzer was a youngster with bold imagination and a strong will, and he needed a challenge.

Opportunities for a career were meager, but he decided to try military service. There was always a war, smaller or larger, and while nobody liked war, a commoner without any means had a chance to make some money as a mercenary soldier. More important for Joseph Pulitzer, a soldier could visit different parts of the world, places where he might find a greater range of opportunity than in the lands of Central Europe. Pulitzer, however, did not have a strong body, and he had bad eyesight. He was rejected three times, first by the Austrians and Prussians, then by the French Foreign Legion, and finally by the English.

With the third rejection, Pulitzer decided to give up and go home. When his ship stopped in Hamburg, he met a recruiter for the Union Army of the United States. The agent may have needed desperately to fill a ship with recruits, for he signed him up. At Boston harbor just before disembarkation Pulitzer swam ashore with a friend, went straight to New York, and enlisted in the First New York Cavalry Regiment. It was an outfit with a large Hungarian contingent.

At the age of 18, a veteran of the Civil War, he went to live and work in the sweatshops of the Austrian-Hungarian and Polish ghettos of New York. But opportunities on the Western frontier had a greater appeal. Pulitzer went to St. Louis where he took odd jobs and spent all his free time in the public library to educate himself in American ways. He took a job as a routine reporter with a German language newspaper, the *Westliche Post.*

As a reporter he found his work restricting and decided that if he owned the paper himself, he could direct editorial policy. To this end he saved his money and bought a part-ownership in the *Westliche Post.* As its publisher, he printed exposes of corruption and quickly discovered that the public was interested in such stories. The paper prospered and in 1878 he was able to sell it and buy a paper published in English, the dwindling *St. Louis Dispatch,* which he combined with the *Evening Post* to form the *St. Louis Post-Dispatch.*

Pulitzer entered newspaper publishing when papers were becoming livelier and more readable. He realized that he could develop this trend by taking advantage of his insight into the times. Immigration was a dominant fact of American life; Pulitzer saw the possibility of making the immigrants regular newspaper readers, which many had not been in Europe. In the columns of his paper he supported causes that affected the lives of this mass of new readers.

A newspaper to Pulitzer was a public trust and not just a private enterprise. Each story should be a contest for the reader and should be written with "accuracy, terseness, accuracy." With this philosophy and method, the *St. Louis Post-Dispatch* became (and remains) a flourishing institution.

In 1883 Pulitzer left the management of the *Post-Dispatch* in other hands, and bought the *New York World.* One of his first steps was to sell the daily for two cents instead of the competitive three and four cents. He undertook an ambitious editorial program. Besides exposing corruption in government, he supported such reforms as a graduated income tax and government regulation of big business, and opposed a protective tariff. His efforts brought him many enemies as well as friends. His critics opposed his political views and claimed that his methods were too sensational — that he practiced "yellow journalism."

In 1947 the United States Government issued a stamp to note the 100th anniversary of the birth of Joseph Pulitzer.

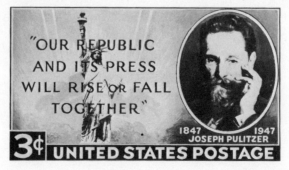

"OUR REPUBLIC AND ITS PRESS WILL RISE OR FALL TOGETHER"

1847 1947
JOSEPH PULITZER

3¢ UNITED STATES POSTAGE

With his hard-working leadership, the *New York World* became one of the outstanding newspapers of its day. But overwork, and lack of sleep and regular meals, weakened Pulitzer's health. He spent the last 20 years of his life a chronic invalid, traveling around in his yacht. He remained, nevertheless, the power behind the *World* right up to his death in 1911.

Pulitzer left a donation of two million dollars to Columbia University to establish a graduate school of journalism. Today his name is most readily associated with the Pulitzer prizes which he inaugurated. In his will he established the prizes "for the encouragement of public service, public morals, American literature and the advancement of education." The prizes are presented annually to American writers, artists, and journalists by the Columbia University on the recommendation of the advisory board of the Pulitzer School of Journalism.

4. *Literature*

A number of Hungarian-Americans have published books in America. They have written significant books in many fields — history, politics, medicine, anthropology, psychiatry, engineering, music. There are fewer works of fiction. A writer usually needs his native tongue for the artistic and intimate use of language in fiction. And many works — especially poetry — are not easily or adequately translated into another language. The Hungarian writer, at home or abroad, has created a distinguished body of literature throughout the centuries. Many of these works have yet to be translated and enjoyed by non-Hungarians.

There is, however, one Hungarian novelist and playwright who stands out in the history of the American theatre. He is Ferenc Molnar (1878-1952), who wrote first in his native Hungarian before his works were translated into English. He was part of a "Hungarian Invasion" of the New York theatre, in the years between 1908 and 1940.

Ferenc Molnar (1878-1952). Among his comedies are *The Guardsman, The Swan,* and *The Play's the Thing.*

In this span of time, 17 Hungarian playwrights had a total of 53 plays produced in New York. The plays — satire, melodrama, farce — were translated and adapted before they were produced for American audiences. Many of the stories expressed the native flavor of Hungarian life and revealed nuances of the Hungarian temperament.

Ferenc Molnar was considered the master of the Hungarian playwrights. He was a fashionable and urbane writer who delighted audiences with his witty dialogue and his skill as a storyteller. His most famous play, *Liliom,* later provided the plot for the Rodgers and Hammerstein musical *Carousel.* In 1940 Molnar came to America and became a permament resident.

Attila the Hun leads his tribe into battle. (*Illustration from Kate Seredy's*
The White Stag, published in 1937 by the Viking Press)

Two other writers of Hungarian background are widely known
by the American public. Edna Ferber was of Hungarian stock;
her father was born in Hungary, her mother in Wisconsin. A natural
storyteller, many of her novels were made into popular movies —
Cimarron, Show Boat, Saratoga Trunk, and *Giant.* For her best-
selling novel, *So Big,* she received a Pulitzer prize in 1924. Miss
Ferber died in 1968, at the age of 82.

Kate Seredy has long delighted young readers with her skillful
writing and masterful illustrations. Several of her most popular
works make use of her Hungarian background. Miss Seredy was
born in Budapest and came to American in 1922. *The Good Master*
is a lively story about country festivals and the life on a Hungarian
farm in the years before World War I. For *The White Stag,* a legend-
ary story about the Hungarian past, she received the 1938 New-
berry Medal awarded to the best children's book of the year.

Author-illustrator **Kate Seredy**, 1930.

5. *Entertainment*

The American motion picture industry was born at the beginning of the century. Numerous personal success stories were a result of its amazing growth, as well as stories of struggles that ended in unfulfilled or shattered dreams.

Two men who illustrate each side of the coin are Adolph Zukor and William Fox, American producers born in Hungary. Each was instrumental in bringing the movie industry into the world of big business. Zukor's long career is associated with Paramount Pictures. William Fox is linked with 20th Century Fox, as his company merged in 1935 with 20th Century Pictures.

Adolph Zukor was one of the first to envision the immense business potential of films and to take steps in its development. He is credited with having produced the first full-length film, *The Prisoner of Zenda,* in 1913. He saw the importance of continually improving the quality of films to keep public interest high.

Many movie magnates have had great financial power, especially in the 1930's. In that era, Zukor's power enabled him to appear on a list—though a controversial one—of the "64 men who ruled the country." In the 1950's, 14 of his films were rated among the Best Hundred of the decade. Zukor is Chairman of the Board at Paramount Pictures, and because of his long and prominent association with films has been called "Mr. Motion Pictures."

The career of William Fox paralleled Zukor's, but only in the 1920's and 1930's. His company rented and later produced films, and owned scores of theatres around the country. His initial investment of $1,700 grew to a 300-million dollar enterprise.

Fox's empire fell apart when the stock market crashed in 1929. He never regained it. Many of his remaining years were devoted to legal battles over bankruptcy problems, which sent him to jail for a year. He died in New York—"not powerful but not poor"— in 1952 of a heart attack.

George Cukor (left) and **Michael Curtiz**. Cukor, a skilled director of high comedy, received an Academy Award for *My Fair Lady* in 1964. The Hungarian-born Curtiz (1898-1962) directed films in Europe before joining Warner Brothers in 1927. *Casablanca* brought him an Oscar in 1943.

Many Hungarians have participated in film-making as scenario writers, directors, actors, and actresses. George Cukor, George Pal, and Joseph Pasternak are noted producers and directors. Two Hungarian actors in earlier films were Bela Lugosi and Peter Lorre. Lugosi was the movies' Dracula. Peter Lorre was a mild, soft-spoken star of horror films and a notable supporting actor in such great films as *Casablanca* and *The Maltese Falcon*.

Adolph Zukor,
head of Paramount Films

Actor Peter Lorre
(1904-1964)

An actor whose career has run from the days of silent films up to the present is Paul Lukas, known for his suave, continental manner. He was a successful actor on stage in Hungary before coming to America. He acted in silent films, and the fact that he could barely speak English did not, of course, interfere with his performance. Then came the crisis of conversion to "talkies." It could have ended his career. But Lukas hired a high school boy to give him English lessons and he learned the language well enough to keep his job. Lukas has appeared in a long list of films and Broadway plays. He played the lead in both the stage and screen productions of *Watch on the Rhine,* and for his role in the film version received an Academy Award (1943).

Paul Lukas studied theatre in Budapest where he made his stage debut in 1916, appearing in the title role of Ferenc Molnar's *Liliom.*

Tony Curtis

Another popular actor of Hungarian background is Tony Curtis. Although he grew up in a tough neighborhood in New York, he was able to free himself, in his words, from "near delinquency" and become an actor. He followed in the footsteps of his father, who had been an actor in Budapest.

Tony Curtis is recognized by many critics as a versatile and dedicated actor, at home in both serious and comic roles (*The Defiant Ones, Some Like It Hot*). In 1958 the Hollywood Foreign Press Association named him "the world's favorite movie actor."

Ernie Kovacs, like Tony Curtis, was born in New York of Hungarian parents. He became a famous television comedian acclaimed for his inventive, unrestrained comedy. Also versatile, he often wrote and produced his own shows. For the 1956-57 television season he received three Emmy Awards. His career was cut short in 1961 when, at the age of 42, he was killed in an automobile accident.

70

Three sisters, Eva, Magda, and Zsa Zsa Gabor, are perhaps more readily associated with their Hungarian background than any other Hungarian-born performers in this country. Eva is a television star and Zsa Zsa appears in films and on television. Zsa Zsa has become noted for her lively personality and her original comments on a variety of subjects. She was reared with her sisters in wealthy surroundings in Hungary, but nevertheless has been said to admire the everyday life. As for her own role, she is quoted in a 1958 interview as saying: "I am the only girl I know who is working her way down instead of up. When I was a little girl I was brought up like a princess; now I am working down to be a chorus girl. Other girls start out as chorus girls and become princesses."

Zsa Zsa Gabor

6. *Art and Design*

Gyorgy Kepes is a writer, teacher, and painter who is widely appreciated for his philosophical writings on art. His books, *Education of Vision, Language of Vision, The New Landscape in Art and Science,* are stimulating works, especially for artists and art teachers. Kepes is Professor of Design at the Massachusetts Institute of Technology.

In art history, Pal Kelemen and Charles de Tolnay have done notable work. Keleman is a leading authority on pre-Columbian art. Two of his books on the subject are *Battlefields of the Gods* and *Medieval American Art.* He has also written a book on the painter El Greco. Charles de Tolnay is an authority on Michelangelo and has published five volumes on this Renaissance artist.

Two American artists of Hungarian birth are Zoltan Sepeshy and Gabor Peterdi. Sepeshy came to America after the first World War. He painted houses and billboards and worked as a window trimmer, a layout artist, and an architectural draftsman before he had his chance as an exhibiting painter. Today many leading museums own his paintings. He is President of the Cranbrook Academy of Art in Bloomfield Hills, Michigan.

Gabor Peterdi, printmaker, is also represented in art collections around the country. He has written two books on prints, *The Basic Procedures of Etching* and *Printmaking.* He lives in Connecticut and teaches at Yale University.

One of the leading architects and designers in America is Hungarian-born Marcel Lajos Breuer. He is called a frontiersman of modern American architecture; many of his pioneering ideas came from his training in Europe. At the Bauhaus in Germany during the 1920's he learned the significance of combining "pure art" with "everyday art" or with functional craftsmanship. Teachers at the Bauhaus believed that houses and chairs could be considered pure art just as can painting or sculpture.

Marcel Breuer (right) examines the plans for one of his buildings at St. John's University, Collegeville, Minnesota.

Marcel Breuer adapted this principle to American technology, which was mass-producing useful objects. His tubular steel chair, designed in 1925, is considered by many critics to be one of the most influential furniture inventions of the century.

As an architect, Breuer has an uncanny gift for making a complex medium seem simple. His clean, box-like forms are the essence of simplicity, as is his use of natural materials like wood and fieldstone. In his words, "I like to use material so its own spiritual peculiarity is visible." For him, wood, fieldstone—even steel—have beauty and should be used, exposed, and enjoyed for themselves as well as for their structural function.

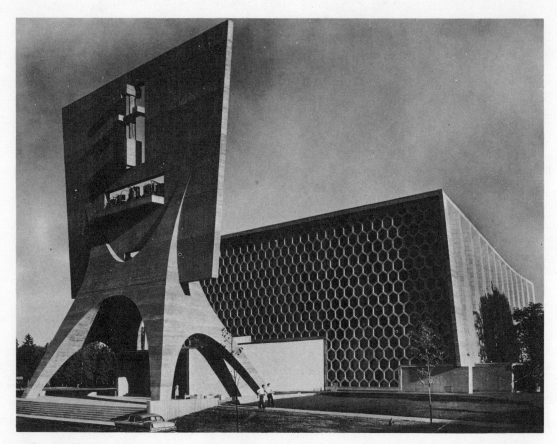

The church at St. John's Abbey, Collegeville, Minn. Breuer's work at St. John's includes a science center and several buildings which make up the Institute for Ecumenical and Cultural Research.

He applied this idea also to the use of concrete, which rarely was thought beautiful in itself. It was considered chiefly a building material that should be hidden or covered. Breuer's use of exposed concrete is amply evident in the church at St. John's Abbey and University in Collegeville, Minnesota. He has designed other buildings on the campus — the library, the science hall, and the dormitories — but the originality and scope of the church remain the most noteworthy. It is acclaimed as one of the finest architectural achievements of our time and as one of America's most significant contributions to church design.

In 1966 the Whitney Museum of American Art moved from 54th Street to its new building on Madison Avenue, designed by Marcel Breuer. (*Photograph courtesy of the Whitney Museum of American Art, 945 Madison Avenue, New York, N.Y.*)

Conclusion

John F. Kennedy in his book *A Nation of Immigrants* quotes the historian, Oscar Handlin, on the vital role of the immigrant in the story of America. Handlin said: "Once I thought to write a history of the immigrant in America. Then I discovered that the immigrants *were* American history."

The story of the Hungarian immigrant is not a separate tale but a thread woven intricately into an American pattern. From the beginning, factory hands and freedom fighters, hussars and heroes, scientists, musicians, and artists—all have given their particular talents to build a new land, which has also become their land. Qualities of diligence, adaptability, and citizenship have made each Hungarian a member of a respected "American family"—the family of Hungarians in America.

...INDEX...

ACKNOWLEDGEMENTS

The illustrations are reproduced through the courtesy of: pp. 6, 9, 31, 33 (top and bottom), 34, 40, A History of Hungary in Biographical Sketches; pp. 10, 24 (right), Dictionary of American Portraits, Dover Publications, Inc.; p. 11, Confederation Life Collection; p. 14, State Historical Society of Wisconsin; pp. 17, 18, 25, 32, 35, 41, 42 (top and bottom), 45, 48, 49, 65, Independent Picture Service; p. 19, Chicago Historical Society; pp. 20, 24 (left), 57, Library of Congress; pp. 22, 63, Post Office Department, Division of Philately; p. 26, Louisiana State University; pp. 27, 29, United States Signal Corps Photo (Brady Collection) in the National Archives; p. 28, American Hungarian Federation; p. 36, United States Immigration and Naturalization Service; p. 46, Yivo Institute for Jewish Research; pp. 51 (top and bottom), 71, Metro-Goldwyn-Mayer, Inc.; p. 53, California Institute of Technology; pp. 54, 55 (top right), Princeton University; p. 55 (top left), Information Division, University of California, Berkeley; p. 55 (bottom), Brandeis University; p. 56 (left), Institute for Muscle Research; p. 56 (right), Harvard University News Office, Cambridge, Massachusetts; p. 59, Hurok Concerts, Inc.; p. 60 (top), Cleveland Orchestra; p. 60 (bottom), Adrian Siegel; p. 61, St. Louis Post-Dispatch; p. 66 (top and bottom), Viking Press; pp. 68 (top left and top right), 69, Warner Brothers; p. 68 (bottom left), Paramount Pictures Corporation; p. 68 (bottom right), Del's Book Service, Norwalk, California; p. 70, United Artists Corporation; pp. 73, 74, St. John's University; p. 75, Whitney Museum of American Art.

ABOUT THE AUTHORS...

REZSOE GRACZA received his basic education in engineering and economics in his native Hungary. Leaving Europe after World War II, he came to the United States and became himself a "Hungarian in America." In 1956 he became a naturalized citizen.

For several years Mr. Gracza was employed in the research enterprises of the flour milling industry. He is the author of more than 30 publications including several patents on industrial processes, particle size technology, and physical chemistry. He is a contributing author of the book *Starch: Chemistry and Technology*. Currently, Mr. Gracza is a manager of design and development projects in a Minneapolis engineering firm.

MARGARET GRACZA is a graduate of Macalester College in St. Paul. She attended the Danish Graduate School for Foreign Students in Copenhagen, Denmark, on a Fulbright scholarship. She worked as a staff member at the International Institute in St. Paul (a recreational and social work agency) and has taught both art and English in high school.

Mrs. Gracza is now a part time writer with the Education Department of the Minneapolis Institute of Arts where she has also served as a museum guide and teacher. She has traveled to several European countries and recently made a trip to Hungary. She is the author of *The Ship and the Sea In Art* and *The Bird In Art*.

The Graczas reside with their son and daughter in Minnetonka, Minnesota.